Who Am I?
and
Where Am I Going?

HOW TO BE AN ANGEL IN
OUR WORLD OF MANY WONDERS

A Great Little Handbook to
Enrich Your Life

HELENA STEINER-HORNSTEYN

ACTIVALE BOOKS

ACTIVALE BOOKS
P.O. Box 7054
Miami Beach Florida 33154-7054
USA

Email:activale@gmail.com
Website:www.activale.com

Original Angel Drawings by Helena Steiner-Hornsteyn

Cover Design by Daniel Middleton

Productions Printed in the United States of America

ISBN-10: 0-9717168-1-1
ISBN-13: 978-0-9717168-1-0

Library of Congress Control Number 2002090425

Second Edition

*Everyone who is seriously
involved in the pursuit of science
becomes convinced that a Spirit is manifest
in the Laws of the Universe.*

— *Albert Einstein*

To Annika, Arianna, and Mattias

Author's Note

I wrote most of this book several years ago. Then I forgot all about it until recently, when I found it in one of my drawers. I felt I would like to share it with others, because it was all about wonderful life wisdom, and wisdom will never be outdated. It will always remain the best kind of news.

"It Is Up to Me What Is to Be in My Life." This is a good code to live by, not only when you are young and starting out on your life's journey but also when you feel it's time to improve your career or relationship —
or maybe you are simply wondering where to turn next.

Don't be misled by the simplicity of this book. Spiritual truth is always simple — almost like looking at the world through the eyes of a child. Unfortunately, our human intellect has a tendency to believe an elaborate uncertainty before we might accept what is really the truth.

The fact that we are spiritual beings living in a physical body is easy and straightforward. Spirit is for absolutely everyone. All you have to do is to show an open mind and remember we are all here for the purposes of learning and making the best of our lives.

As you read through these pages, you'll find that this is a book packed with life's wisdom. It is not theory but the conclusion of hard-earned experience: I had to find out for myself what works and what doesn't work! It took me many years to understand that this was true. It's amazing how you have to go through certain things again and again before you can accept that your own well-being and life

situation might actually involve you — and ask for action of your own.

A great part of my life was filled with wealth and fun parties. I loved my life, and everyone was so nice and friendly to my face. But as time went by, I began to question the validity of that lifestyle and began to look for "something more" to give my life a deeper meaning.

To my amazement, I received much more than I had ever imagined, although times were not always easy.

In the end, I was grateful for the many new and interesting experiences. Mind you, I wasn't grateful when I was right in the middle of those so-called "interesting" times, and it would have been easy to blame the world and everyone else for what was happening to me. The reward comes only after you have found the truth — when you can look back and understand how and why it all happened.

I have found that Attitude plus an Unconditional Open Mind is the founding formula to make your life a more exciting and worthwhile one. In a way, we may have chosen, directly and indirectly, where we find ourselves right now.

Read slowly and enjoy the book. As you read through these pages, if you should be reminded of something wonderful in your life, stay with that good thought for a while, and know that life can be full of many, many more fantastic times.

— *Helena Steiner-Hornsteyn*
Miami Beach, Florida

How It Began

We all lived in the Land of Big Heart,
where we had been taught
to be part of a safe and protected life,
how to speak to each other,
how to think about each other,
and
how work and play with each other.
Life was moving along.
We had what we needed to live a good life.
And we were dancing and laughing
with each other.
Day after day…
year after year…
from morning to night.

Yes, we lived our days the same way
we had done forever in our land.
We sang songs with words
that we all knew by heart,
and we sang them again and again.
And again.
Just like others had done
long, long before us —
not looking for anything to be changed.
Why bother? we said.
It's easier this way.
Let's stay with the same song
we have all known for so long.

1

A few times the Land of the Big Heart
was hit by bad times.
The sky then turned grey
as the storms blew in among our midst.
And we stopped dancing,
because
we now had to listen to a new tune.
Obediently, we followed new rules and
began to march:
One... two...
one... two... one... two....

We watched the sky as the
thunder rumbled above our world,
and bolts of lightning exploded before our eyes.
The ground was trembling under our feet.
And we were whispering to each other —
not daring to sing
because we had not yet been told
which words would be the right words to use.

This will pass, we said behind our closed doors.
Of course it will.
The storm will soon disappear all by itself.

And indeed, as time went by,
the sun was shining again,
drying the ground from water
and all the old mess.

And after awhile,
all was forgotten, and
the memories of the grey skies,
the thunder, the lightning,
and the marches
were all gone.
And it didn't take long
until
we were dancing again.
Laughing and singing
the same old songs
as they had always been sung before.
We saw only those same things
we had always seen before.
And we said and thought the same things
we had always said before.
There was no reason to change those ways.
No reason at all.

Transition

Time went by.
One year was added to the other.
Then one day —
suddenly, and to my surprise...
I,
little me,
little unknown me,
stood up and said:
I don't want to dance anymore.
And I want to sing no more of those old songs
I have heard so many times before.
And I am sick and tired of laughing —
I am looking for a CHANGE in my life.
A REAL change this time.
I think I want to explore
and look around for a while.

Explore? Look around?
You said "look for a change"?
What do you mean by that?
You want to laugh and dance no more?
Not think and do like we do?
You tell us you don't want to belong anymore?
Why? Why? Why?

No reason why;
only
I feel that somewhere, beyond the horizon,
there must be a world of much, much MORE.
A place where you can walk in and out.
Jump high and sideways.
Try out new words and new tunes —
a place where I dare sing a new song.
Even dare try not one but MANY new songs —
I think I have heard of a place called UNIVERSE.

Universe?
What is "Universe"?
We don't understand.
It doesn't sound like "US,"
and it doesn't fit into our land.
So go away.
Try your new world called Universe,
and never dance with us again!

Amazed, I said nothing
as they lifted me off my feet.
There was no word to be heard as
I was carried to the heights of the City wall
and pushed over the rim
into the thin air.
Away from the limits of Big Heart,
and what I had always called "home"
was home no more.

As I fell through the air,
I could still hear their laughter
echoing through my ears
and the words of the same songs I had heard
so many, many
times before.
I knew from that moment,
I was already forgotten.

With my hands and arms
I tried to find something in the empty air
to grab and hang on to for my life.
But I realized there was nothing there
but just me —
my little, little self.
And I kept falling and falling…
and then, suddenly,
in the middle of the air,
I stopped falling.

The Next Level

Baffled, I looked around.
Nothing was there to hold me up
but just ME —
little, little ME.
Right there in the middle of the sky.
And suddenly, it dawned on me:
I COULD FLY!
Excited, I tried my new strength,
making loops
and making turns
to the left and to the right.
And I noticed I could fly any direction
I had the wish to go.

Startled,
I touched my back
and to my surprise,
I found I had
WINGS!

Wings?
Yes wings !
All of a sudden it dawned upon me:
I was an Angel!

Angel?
Me — an Angel?
But why? Why? Oh why?
What is an Angel?
What do Angels do?
What do Angels say?
Where do Angels live?
Where do Angels come from?

As I asked myself those questions,
an incredible feeling of calm surged through my body.
And then I understood:
Somewhere along the line, I had made a choice
according to my open mind,
and my new home was now to be found
right in my heart.
Finally —
I was now free to explore
and
to look around
for
more — even much
MORE.

Immediately after I realized
that I was an Angel,
I jumped up into the sky,
ready to enjoy my new-found freedom.
And as I flew through the skies
looking at the world below,
I discovered my eyes were more open
than they ever were before.
I now saw more:
"sideways and beyond."
And I knew the reason for this was
I had been given the gift
of an
Open Mind
to understand
what it was all about.

With joy in my heart
I discovered
"IMPROVISE."
Because when you open your mind,
you discover so much more,
and never-ending possibilities
are given to your receiving hands.
So you can try and try —
each time in a different way.

As I moved along,
I thought it would be easy for an Angel
to find That Paradise
I earlier had believed was
the Perfect Conclusion
of all and everything.
But I had to think again,
because I had found
that
in the Paradise we call Perfection,
there is
Absolutely Everything!
And I found that
the Downs
are as much part of the Perfection
as are all the Ups and the In-betweens!

Next step is to
experience firsthand
that the Perfection in
YOUR LIFE
is connected to
YOUR ACCEPTANCE and
YOUR TOLERANCE
of things.
This means you have to
stop judging
what you don't understand.

And when you do stop all the judgement,
You begin not only to understand
but also
how to LIVE
the Meaning of Unconditional Love.
It means Judge Not.
It means Letting Go.
It means Looking Ahead and to Move On.
It means Understanding
that we are not exactly the same —
the way we feel and think about things.
This is the way it is,
because some are simply not as ready
or courageous
as others
to dare
GO FOR
those new ideas and adventures
that are hiding on the other side of the Horizon.
And this is still OK.

And an urge to use my new freedom and
ability to fly
to reach for more adventures,
inspiration, and
new opportunities
shivered through my little Angel body.
Wow,
this was going to be such fun!

I was now ready to fly far away
into the Galaxies of
many new stars —
to explore a Universe of
New Views and
New-Found Truths
and to explore what some believed to be
SECRETS.
I knew that my life was ahead of me
and not behind me
and that this Universe, where I now live,
is the key to what is all about ME.

And as I began to fly to many new places
and visited all kinds of new stars of the Universe,
I realized my wings could carry me
much further away
than I ever imagined I could go
because I had left the limitation of
my old flock behind.
And soon
I found there is so much more to discover.
Much more than I ever thought was possible —
even for an Angel.

And I found that when I was happy about my day,
others who were also happy about their day
would come to be with me.
And when I was sad and feeling not so well,
others who also felt sad and low like I did
would come my way.
Even for an Angel —
this was big news.

Sometimes you have to travel very far
to find out
what YOU
are all about.
And when you finally discover
who and what you really are
and
why you are you are here in this world,
you recognize that it was never necessary to
have travelled all that way to find out.
Not necessary at all:
All you needed and wanted to know
was always
RIGHT HERE,
where you have been all along,
because what you really needed to know
was how to find the knowledge of your
Inner Self —
"The Power That Knows All And Sees All."
And this Power is always, always
right where you are....

And now that I have come this far
in my Angel experience,
I still have to stop
believing that, as soon as I had found the
Secret
about my Inner Self,
I would then know everything.
But this is not so.
Once you have found the secret about yourself,
you have to understand HOW TO LIVE this knowledge
and
experience first hand that this is really so....
At the right time.
In the right places.
In the right ways.
Not until then can you say that
you have found the Secret.

I also found that the more knowledge
I acquired as an Angel,
the more I began to feel that my
broadened knowledge was not enough.
Everything was so different from before —
when I lived in the Land of Big Heart.
At that time, I knew just very, very little,
but I still believed
I knew everything there was to know!

The truth is that Knowledge never ends....
The more you open your mind,
the greater the vision
and
the larger you make your territory of wisdom.
This way
more and more knowledge
keeps on coming to you.

The biggest expert of all
Is the one
who
just LOVES
finding out more
and more, and more —
with no limitations or
preset opinions in mind.

Because knowledge is not only
never-ending:
It is Alive.
It unfolds.
It constantly opens new doors
and moves along with time!

Life is a book with many pages and
many new chapters.
You have to keep on turning those pages,
one after the other.
And then you should stop here and there and
reflect a little bit
about "THINGS."

You'll then realize that
"Those Little Things"
probably were much more important
than you thought at first.
And what you once considered Big Things
ended up being not so important after all.

And as you lived through one
triumph (or even blunder) after the other,
you added new riches to your life.
And should the day come
when you sit back and say,
'I now know it all.
I have seen all.'
And you believe there is nothing more
for you to learn...
that is the day you have chosen to
turn your life into the PAST.
And you will grow old,
in spite of the many riches of knowledge
you collected
in your pockets and in your hands.

Before I knew I was an Angel,
I never really understood
WHY I was here on Earth, nor did I understand
the meaning of my life.
I have now come to realize:
My thinking was then
CONDITIONED to be a certain way
because human brain power
has been programmed
to be a certain way and
to go "just so far" —
leaving most of Universe's incredible knowledge
unexplored and untouched!

As an Angel person you
are meant
to connect and
TO BE IN TUNE
continuously
with that
"HIGHER GOOD"
of the Universe
to enrich
Your Life and
to enrich the Lives of Others.

As an Angel you soon find that you cannot reach
the Big Knowledge of the Universe
through your Brain Power alone —
nor through the many words of
knowledge from others.
You, yourself,
have to act and
make the commitment...
and
you have to just
LOVE
DOING SO!

As an Angel, you know WHEN and HOW TO
LISTEN,
particularly
when the HEAVENS are speaking to you.
And you know
that in spite of the many differences
between us all,
we are ALL of the same.
And in the end,
our feelings on
how we care for those we love
will coincide
and
Be One Awareness
and One Love.

Because...

it's so simple:

The Source is only ONE!

And when YOU have received
whatever Good
has come your way,
YOU SAY
THANK YOU
as often as YOU can.
Because in the eyes of Universe,
to give thanks is very, very important.

And when you give,
you give from your heart,
because when you give from your heart,
you give to the Heavens —
and Universe will be the one to reward you.
Not necessarily will you receive your reward
from that one person to whom
you gave your gift.

"Give and you shall be given,"
says the Big Book of old wisdom —
a good rule in the eyes of an Angel.

When you give from your heart
with no conditions or strings attached,
Universe will respond and
be there for you.
In the same way,
when you are given,
learn to receive with joy and appreciation
in your heart!
You will then
TRULY
RECEIVE
the way it was meant to be...

...and not until then will you be part of that
Something More —
of The Big Universe
That Knows All and Sees All.
And the key to finding that Universe
is to be found
within YOU
and
ME
and within each one of us.
And it will determine the way we feel and
think about things and each other,
and most of all...
you'll find out
who you really are.

And when you understand,
what you are all about,
that is the time
you'll understand
WHAT OTHERS ARE ALL ABOUT.
Because not until you love and understand Yourself
can you also love others
the way it was meant to be
when you say
you know and have known love.

You are in total charge of YOU!
Nobody in the whole world is
responsible for you
and your own success
as much as
YOU are responsible
FOR YOU
and
your own success!

Angels know that:
You cannot expect others to
make your life a good life.
ONLY YOU
will make your day a good day,
and you, yourself, are
RESPONSIBLE
to
give it a good
TRY !

It so happens that your life depends on
your choices —
your OWN choices —
as everything else in the world
depends on choices made by others.
You always have the free will to choose
YOUR wish.
Nobody else knows your true wish but you.
And what you choose to do today —
even right now —
could affect your future
one way or another.
Sometimes even totally.

Somewhere in the depth of your soul,
there is a Master Plan for your life.
Your soul knows about this master plan,
and it is
constantly
trying to
remind you of your plan.
This plan is already known to you
as the deep desire of your heart.

BUT…
you have the choice not to listen
to your heart's desires,
if this is what you prefer.
Remember the old saying :
IT IS UP TO ME
what is going to be!

Your choice has to start in YOUR heart.
And this can be the hardest one of all
because it's between
YOU and YOU
and
NOBODY ELSE.
And you have to be so
TOTALLY HONEST
with yourself!

Angels know that there is
YOU —
the body
and
YOU —
Your Spirit.
They are both really you,
and somehow you have to balance the two
and not neglect one for the other!

When you feel a little low,
go hug a TREE
because nature is full of
Universe's own Healing Power!
And you'll find comfort
any time
you agree to be receptive to this unconditional
universal helping source.
You'll be surprised to see
how well it works.

And should you see a little butterfly, or flower,
or little kitten on the way,
remember to send your childlike love.
Because there is always something or
someone out there for you to love.
Love never disappears from life,
particularly not from your life...
even if you feel so at times.

When people try to become Angels,
They might
over-read,
over-study,
and over-pray.
And most of all…
over-expect!
All it takes to be an Angel
is to
keep an open mind —
and
connect with the true feelings of your heart!

The power of Universe
may have many names
depending where you find yourself in the world
and the way you have been taught to think and
feel about things.
However, the power is still the same...
everywhere.
Always !

So everyone

is

Right!

Because Universe is
so much bigger
and
loving
than a human mind
will ever comprehend!

Creation doesn't see imperfection.
Only people
see that way.
Angels remember that in Perfection
there is absolutely
EVERYTHING!

Just like YOU change with time,
so does Nature and the whole Planet,
because both Nature and the Planet
are alive —
just like you are!
What is desert today
was once green and lush.
What is green and lavish today
might one day be desert and forgotten.
And what was cold
turned warm —
sometimes even very warm
or very cold.
And what was the bottom of the ocean
turned into mountains
higher than you could ever imagine.

How very impossible that may seem,
it still happened.
Reality is sometimes so very
unreal
and beyond our comprehension,
so believe
everything is possible.

You cannot predict
When and Why things happen.
Of course you can — and
often you certainly DO.
But God always —
always —
has the final word!

God made no rules of fear and injustice.
MAN made those rules.
Man teaches you to fear.
Man tells you to take sides.
Man tells you of your guilt.
Man makes you believe a certain way.
Man forces you to fight wars
in God's name.
The Truth is that
never — EVER — has God
asked Man to kill
in God's name !

And Man says Man is Man,
and that Woman is Woman,
and that Black is Black,
and that Yellow is Yellow —
and that Purple doesn't belong.
And Man says that Rich is Rich
and Poor is Poor.
And Man tries to decide who is what
to separate us all from another.
God, on the other hand,
says,
"You are all My children.
I love you all the same —
just the way you are!"

Your Faith must never scare you.
If it does,
rub your eyes and
WAKE UP!

It will never be possible for the
Human Intellect
to override Spirit.
Why not?
Because Spirit was there first.
Because Spirit created intellect.
Because Spirit created YOU.
It is that simple.

Or —

Do you have a better idea
for the world to know?

TRUTH
is
QUIET.
Those who shout have to do so
to cover what is quiet.

Somewhere on your journey as an Angel,
you discover that there is no real ending
where you can say
that you are the best of all —
or that you know all
or that you have finished
what was meant for you to do...
and that All is now completed.
Maybe, throughout your whole life,
you have been made to believe that this was so
and even planned to welcome your ending
somewhere in your life —
long before it was time to go.

There is no wall that says
The End
when you have reached a certain age
or accomplishment,
because Life is energy —
and energy is continuous.

'Continuous' means
It Never Ends!
It keeps on going and going...and going.

AND GOING....

SOMEWHERE HALFWAY
through your life,
you may remember there were times
when you experienced
what you thought to be
the best times of your life...
and now you realize:
Those good times were
NOT because of THINGS!

As time passes by, you'll notice
certain things are still there and
have never disappeared from life —
not even from your particular life.
And they may still be
GOOD THINGS
for you to enjoy.

Dreams DO come true.
They just have to be so important to you
that YOU make them happen.

As an Angel, I found
that I don't have to go anywhere
to find
harmony or
love or
success in my life
because all those good things
start right here and
right now
within ME —
and not only within me
but
within you
and
each one of us.
Right here and now.
All we have to do is
to
GET GOING!

Looking back at my life and how I was
thrown over the rim,
away from the security of
the Land of the Big Heart,
I am now grateful
for things
I thought were a burden for me before,
because I now find
how all those Events in my life
all make sense and
how they helped me reach
more knowledge,
more love, and
absolutely more
WISDOM
in my life.

And I now know how
you and I
can be Angels at any time we so desire.
We don't have to wear certain clothes
or go to a special building,
a certain mountain,
or a certain country to get started.
And I know that you and I and
everyone and everything
in the whole wide world
are all united in
a timeless
"Allness of All" —
an Eternity of sharing.
But we may have trouble doing so,
because it could be easier
to pretend and
look the other way.

In my Angel life
I have seen one truth after the other
unfold,
and I realize my awareness has grown —
and so has the depth and width of
my Universe.
And so has our relationship with each other.
Because I now know
that what I have called
UNIVERSE
is very much what
I ALLOW my UNIVERSE TO BE.
And all the riches
that Universe is willing to give to me
are — again —
what I ACCEPT to be given to me.

I, myself, have to do the forgiving and the forgetting.

I, myself, have to take action if I truly wish to win.

I, myself, set the limit on What Is To Be.

Have a great day today.

And make every day a great day.

This book is meant to be read again and again.

Keep it by your bedside side and read it

from time to time.

And reflect for a while....

The particular thoughts you allow to

go through your mind

before you close your eyes for the night

will most likely be the foundation

for the beginning of your next day.

With positive thoughts in your mind,

your new day will be a

much happier and healthier day.

About the Author

Helena Steiner-Hornsteyn, a native of Sweden, is ranked among the top four healers in the world in the field of intuitive healing and spiritual development. She works on the principle that we are energy; that everything around us is energy; and that everything you feel, think, and do is energy — and energy never dies. She holds a Doctorate of Divinity degree and maintains medical intuitive offices in both the United States and Europe.

Before her spiritual calling, Helena was active in the international business world, a busy socialite, and a world traveler. But many extraordinary spiritual experiences finally came to completely change the direction of her life.

She is the founder and former Chairman of the Institute for Positive Living in Berlin and Baden-Baden, Germany; she also founded and served as Chairman of the Board of the Symphony Guild of South Florida, a not-for-profit organization that provides scholarships for exceptional music students and promotes international cultural exchange programs. She also founded and supported two major South Florida symphony orchestras.

A popular international speaker–lecturer, she divides her time between her offices in Europe and the U.S. She is a mother and a grandmother who makes her home in Miami Beach, Florida.

Acknowledgments

I recognize in gratitude that my life and work have been made possible by the continuous and loving persistence of Spirit. I will forever remain grateful for the many new and exciting possibilities that have continually opened up before me — usually when I least expected it, but always reassuring me of the true purpose of my life.

I am also grateful that my life has been touched by so many wonderful and helpful people who believed in my vision and were there for me and to support my endeavors. Without your helping hands, it would not have been possible for me to reach out to so many and be where I am now.

To my beautiful daughter Annika and my lovely grandchildren Arianna and Mattias — thank you for your incredible spiritual awareness and for always being there for me.

Thank you to my friends Wildfrid de Flon, Gunilla von Post, and Sharon Hamilton for always lending me an ear. And thank you for your great help, Seppo Laakso, with family, Sirkku Bjorklund, Titti Gronblom, and Inge Engstrom, Marianne Lival, Era Nova Book Shop and Mina Olen Magazine in Helsinki, Heidi Jonsdalen, and Lisbeth Pettersen. Ola and Rigmor Bruseth, you did so much. Thank you, Tamas Burger in Palm Beach, for your trust and belief in me. Thank you, Dan Danielson, for reading and believing in the manuscript; Christine DeLorey for all your good advice and great knowledge.

We are all shining Lights on
Earth with unlimited
possibilities within us.

www.ingramcontent.com/pod-product-compliance
Lightning Source LLC
Chambersburg PA
CBHW030514100426

42813CB00001B/42